Biography of a Man with a Full Life

J. W.
March 2014

Printed in the United States of America.

ISBN 978-0-9970242-8-9

J Winthrop, Charleston, South Carolina

www.winthropfamily.org

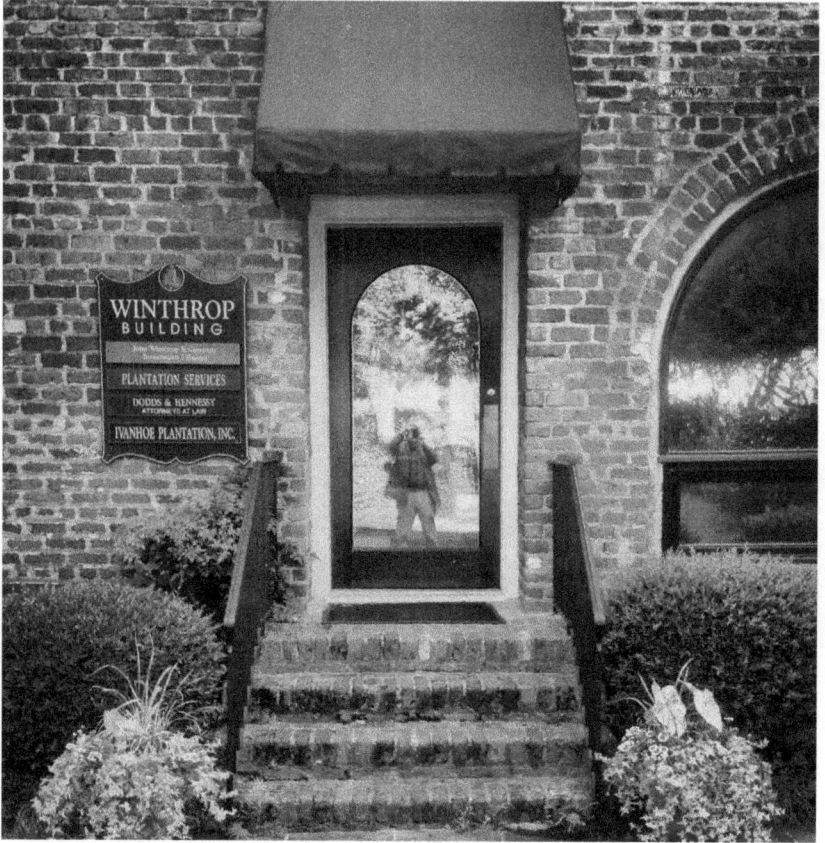

Winthrop Building, Charleston, South Carolina.

John Winthrop was born in Boston and spent his earliest years in Virginia and then Massachusetts, followed by New York. After his parents were divorced in 1945, he moved to New York City and attended the Buckley School. These four years were followed by another four years at Saint Mark's School in Southborough, Massachusetts, and then by four years at Harvard in Cambridge.

With a college degree in hand, he joined the Navy and became a journalist for two years. His formal academic training resumed with two years at Columbia University, where he received an MBA.

During the Kennedy years, he went to Washington, DC, once again as a journalist for *The Atlantic Council*, followed by a trip around the world while writing for *The Boston Globe*.

Marriage (two times), a tour of duty on Wall Street, and a move to Charleston, South Carolina, followed.

All of this can be understood in more detail by glancing through the pages of his memories, published as part of a collection for his sons and grandchildren in 2012 under the title *I Remember the Robins Chirping*.

Groton Plantation Family Meeting.

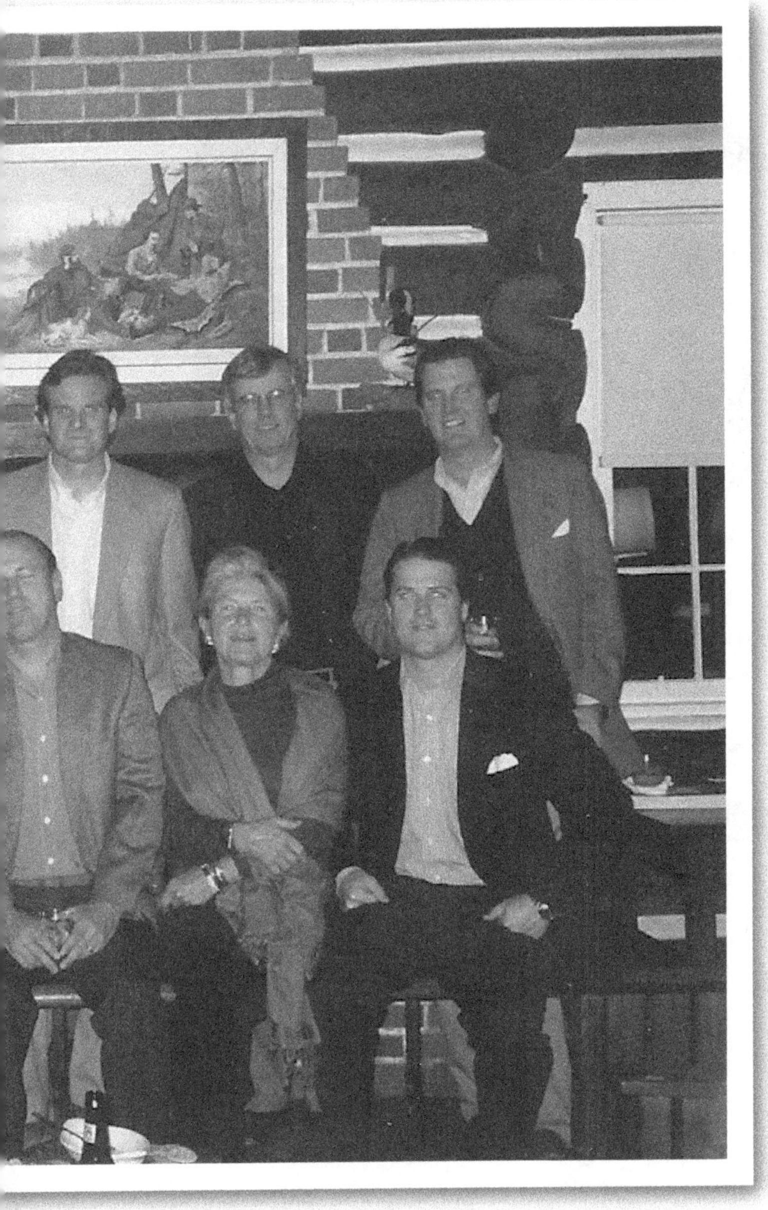

John "Jay" Winthrop, Jr.

Louisa and Gren Winthrop.

Bayard and father John Winthrop.

Baby Agnes with father Bayard Winthrop, Lakeville.

Edward Field "Teddy" Winthrop,
graduation from Salsbury School, 2005.

Matthew Bartlett Winthrop (1938 - 2013)

Young John Winthrop with baby brother Matthew, Manchester, Massachusetts, 1939.

JW and EGW, London, 2013
(after hearing Ambassador Matthew Winthrop Barzun
give a Thanksgiving address at St. Paul's.)

a few recollections of my

- I remember the robins chirping in the early spring as I went to sleep in our grandparents' safe and secure home in Beverly Farms, Massachusetts.

- My fourth birthday party at my grandparents' home – the frosting on the cake was pink and a toy jack-knife was my most treasured present.

- Walks on Singing Beach in Manchester, Massachusetts, with my brother, Matthew, and our mother.

- The itchy woolen leggings I was forced to wear in Boston by our nurse – a very evil woman. She seemed to enjoy giving us the taste of soap as well.

- Pounding tennis balls into open windows of our second home called Stone Lea in Manchester. Matthew was an expert at this sport.

- The separation and ultimate divorce of our parents.

earliest years . . .

- Our father away in the Navy fighting the German and Japanese enemies while I traced the progress of the Allied Forces on a map at our home in Manchester, Massachusetts. A picture of a B-29 bomber decorated the wall of my bedroom.

- Mack, our tutor, helping us with carpentry projects.

- "Spats," (a severe slap with a wooden paddle) dished out for punishment by Dave Kliever, ex-Marine.

- Fishing off the rocks of our beachfront home in Manchester.

- Riding the waves in Singing Beach – our greatest joy at the time.

- Getting stung by a bee in the mouth on Singing Beach, and, a few days later, falling down a rocky cliff outside our home. I cried for a long time after each of these events.

from days in Boston,

- Our difficult adjustment after the divorce of our parents.

- The early days at Dexter School, entering the third grade (with Matthew in first grade).

- Matthew competing with John Nelson for an academic prize in mathematics.

- The love of baseball and the joy of my achievement as a young boy at Dexter (breaking the throwing record for the "Midget" baseball competition).

- The terrifying experience of having to report to the headmaster (after kicking off my shoe and breaking a lamp by mistake while imitating the Nazi goose step).

- Playing football in the gray sweater of the Mohawk team in sports at Dexter school.

- Feeling enormous empathy for Matthew, who tipped over backward and lost much blood from cracking his head on the radiator at our home.

remember . . .

- Going to Harvard with classmate John Finley
  and being brought to Winthrop House by
  his famous father, Professor Finley.

- Wearing red Dexter hats on the bus to school
  from our home on Marlboro Street.

- Matthew's snowball attack on a McKann
  car limousine outside our home in
  Boston (infuriating the driver).

- Drawing pictures of U.S. airplanes attacking
  Japanese zeros with classmate Harry Thayer.

- Getting my first camera as a Christmas
  present from Aunt Theo.

from New York and Buck-

- Our introduction to our new home at 770 Park Avenue, where we were to live with our father and "Miss Dice" – a governess.

- The wonder of seeing cars passing far below our fifth floor apartment on Park Avenue.

- The arrival of wonderful Aunt Nina (Countess Moltke), who was to help shape my early years in this new home.

- The arrival of my dog Tessie, who was to be my full responsibility and who became a devoted pet. (She eventually died while I was in the Navy.)

- Early days at Buckley with friends Curtiss Scarritt, Hayden Conner, Bill Mateleine, Pierre de Vegh, and many more.

- Dodge ball and "battlefield" at Buckley, my favorite sports at the time, along with baseball.

ey School, I remember . . .

- Difficulty with homework in mathematics
  followed by frustrating tutorials with our father
  who was so accomplished at math and physics,
  while I experienced problems with both.

- Trips to Uncle Bob and Aunt Meg's pool in the
  summer time (they rarely appeared on the scene).

- A trip to Bermuda on the *Queen of Bermuda* with
  Mr. Toemey, Harold Block, and Pierre de Vegh
  – with occasional vomits in our stateroom caused
  by seasickness. (This was not a joyful trip!).

- Hurling toys and grapefruits out of Curtiss Scarritt's
  window, causing horror and chaos below.

- Saturday Club and Cub Scout meetings
  (to keep young boys out of trouble).

- The marriage of our father to
  Eleanor Beane from Boston.

from Saint Mark's School,

- The feeling of having to make it on my own in a new place, while a new family was being created by my father and Eleanor.

- My inability to compete with the best of Saint Mark's baseball players.

- A solid friendship with Curtiss Scarritt – the only fellow transplant from Buckley, aside from John J. Mortimer.

- The discovery of an unexpected talent within myself in wrestling, followed by three years of undefeated varsity competition. This seemed like a big deal at the time, and made up for my failure in baseball.

- Fixation on grades, grades, grades, so I could get into a decent college.

- The spiritual side of life took on new meaning (along with confirmation in the church).

- Letters from Suzy Ray, my first girlfriend, were treasured for a while along with frequent letters from our mother.

I remember . . .

- Being elected captain of the wrestling team built some self confidence, along with a letter in soccer. So much for sports.

- Summer visits to Beverly Farms and a growing fondness of for my stepfather, Bartlett Harwood, gave me a sense of direction and support I needed. This was about the only time Matthew and I could play and bond together during our teenage years.

- Acceptance to Harvard was a nice reward at the end of my four difficult years at St. Mark's.

- I left the school with an unexpected prize – the Seton Porter reward for tenacity and for best fulfilling the school motto – *Age Quod Agis* – (Do what you do well). What a nice memory that was!

- While my mother loved me and spoiled me, she made me give the $100 which came with the Seaton Porter prize to Saint Mark's as a gift.

and from Harvard . . .

- Freshman year in Wigglesworth with many new friends and some outrageous incidents. It was about this time that Matthew dropped out of Solebury School.

- Mortimer, Davis and Church pointing an ROTC rifle at innocent street walkers, while Wagnerian music played loudly in the background.

- Bob Montgomery's early marriage to Ginger Patterson, followed by a drunken brawl weekend starring John Davis and Dan Morgan.

- Winning the freshman wrestling honors, but losing a few on the Harvard varsity team.

- Election to all the leading clubs, but deciding on Porcellian after weighing Bart's and Lou McCagg's advice. This seemed so important at the time.

- Various jobs taken to support the Porcellian Club bills (at our father's insistence) at Dexter School as a coach; at J. August, a clothier, packing suits; and, finally, selling Cutco cutlery door-to-door. My father held me to a very strict budget. I always tried to please him.

- Struggling with my work – especially
  in the beginning (in our small English
  comp class, Erich Segal was a star).

- Trips to Cuba, to Russia, to Bermuda, and
  to Lana Labelle Farm in Pennsylvania,
  created bonding relationships.

- These were the golden years for Groton Plantation,
  where my father generously allowed me to invite
  many friends, shoot quail and raise hell.

- Two friends, George Ellison and Godfrey Truslow
  (both now deceased), almost got me kicked out of
  Harvard for reasons I wish I was at liberty to disclose.

- Treasuring the solid relationship of
  friends at Harvard, including Heard,
  Clark, Krogh, Davis and others.

- More trips to Groton Plantation in my spare time
  and, finally, acceptance into the U.S. Navy.

from the days in the U.S.

- Dreaming of becoming an officer on our aircraft carrier in the Pacific.

- Reporting for duty and OCS two weeks after graduation.

- Growing difficulties in Newport with the realization that graduates were heading for the Atlantic-based destroyers.

- Accepting the painful decision to flunk and rationalize that I would become a better officer after experiencing the rigors of being an enlisted man.

- Going to boot camp in Great Lakes – lead man on the hose fighting a fire – strep throat in the infirmary.

- Assignment to destroyer tender Sierra AD 18 out of Norfolk (the same ship that carried my father home from WW II).

Navy . . .

- Writing the ship's newspaper and eventually hosting my own radio program. Meanwhile, brother Matthew was writing me many cards and letters, as was a girlfriend, our mother and Aunt Nina.

- Mediterranean Cruise and upgrading to Journalist Third Class.

- Guantanamo Bay cruise after liberty on Virginia Beach on weekends.

- Fear of war over Berlin as we were ordered to go on a transatlantic cruise on the USS Sierra (AD-18).

- The joy of receiving an honorable discharge and acceptance into Columbia MBA program.

- Launching an amateur's career in broadcasting and journalism – both of which provided a creative outlet in the years to come.

business school years and

- Difficulty with Professor Bastable in Accounting & Statistics.

- Satisfaction in Manpower essay with Professor Ginsberg.

- St. Anthony Hall (a fraternity) as a refuge and as an eating club.

- Small apartment uptown on West Side as first perch.

- Kennedy inaugural on TV in 1960 ... a very exciting time.

- Summer job at Citibank in London job with George Parker and Kelly Anderson.

Washington . . .

- Butler as roommate in second year.

- Atlantic Council job with Christian Herter and Cabot Lodge, and move to Washington, DC.

- Occasional breakfast in the White House during the Kennedy years.

- Marriage to Deborah in Sewickley, Pennsylvania.

- Trip around world before settling in New York and writing a series of articles for *The Boston Globe* – a major event before going to Wall Street!

- Acceptance of a job at Wood, Struthers & Winthrop, necessitating a departure from Washington, DC.

- Began seeing more of brothers, but realizing more and more that Matthew might require special attention.

WSW and divorce . . .

- First day of work in January with Steve Schwartz as roommate (and $5,000 annual pay).

- Difficulty in research department under Galban and Jones.

- Bob Wood's tutelage in investment advisory department, introducing me to more interesting work.

- Attentive to R.W. and R. George, fearful of G. Copp and Oakley Brooks, friendly with nearly all co-workers.

- Blackout night in 1969 – long walk uptown to get home.

- Unable to control my wife's spending spree and other problems at home.

- Served with papers for divorce.

- Peter French and Sam LaFace as indispensible friends along with Arthur Field.

- Admission as a partner, leading to a leadership role in the investment advisory department. (Sherry before lunch on Mondays was always a high point!)

- Rapid decline of the other segments of business at WS&W, and eventual merger with DLJ, after consideration of F.S. Mosley, White Weld and other possible merger candidates at the time.

- Meanwhile – through all of this – broadening of my perspective through board work on Green Bay & Western Railroad, NUI Utility, Groton Land Company, and Wood, Struthers & Winthrop ... also in the not-for-profit arena, Fresh Air Fund, Saint Mark's, Greenwich Country Day School and Educational Policy Center, among others.

- Having completed the merger of our firm and a painful divorce, I began to think about new opportunities, among them developing a special niche with trustee assignments at four mutual fund management companies.

- Most important of all – the arrival of three sons who I knew I would love unconditionally always!

- An over-arching responsibility for Matthew and to a very real extent, the broader family as well.

memories of Charleston . . .

- Digesting the fear of a culture shock after deciding to move to Charleston with only three friends in the city (Messrs. Ravenel, Duell, and Manigault).

- Realizing almost immediately that a balance in life between for-profit involvement and not-for-profit involvement gave me a more complete feeling.

- Serving on at least fifteen boards in each category and running a few entities in each created a signal ... not to boast about any achievements – particularly in my adopted city!

- It is axiomatic that achievements or opinions brought to the Holy City are of limited interest (as it is elsewhere!).

- A commitment to the community by outsiders is of interest.

- Gradually finding a level of acceptance only if we behaved ourselves. New doors began to open up in Charleston.

- Moved from 52 King Street to 9 Ladson Street. We built a Widow's Walk on top of our new house.

- Purchased a commercial building at One North Adger's Wharf, intended as an investment for my sons as well as for me. It also provided a place to work following Hurricane Hugo.

- Our new home became a target for gatherings of various not-for-profit events, for parties, for club and society gatherings.

- Monthly visits to see Matthew in Boston became a scheduled project along with business and charity trips to New York.

- A major effort was made to connect with my own family which became more and more challenging as they settled elsewhere.

- With all the good things that developed in Charleston, we missed the cooler weather in the summer and the limited choices in education. We also missed our friends and family.

children . . . . a series of

- Dr. Martens introducing me to my eldest son.

- Jay and Gren meet in New York apartment for the first time (after Gren's birth).

- Bayard's arrival in Greenwich Hospital delivery room (my only son born in New England).

- Teddy's yawn upon his first encounter with me.

- Groton Plantation hunts with BB guns, rifles, and shotguns.

- Jay's near drowning incident in our neighbor's pool.

- Gren's near catastrophe with a car running over him.

- Bayard's weight problem ... and then a gradual recovery.

- Drugs, motor scooter, cars, and alcohol worries of all four sons continuing with Teddy (born in June of 1986).

- Jay's entry into the "war zone" of money management, setting up his own firm with Rob Douglass, while Gren and Bayard followed suit by setting up their own companies in Charleston and San Francisco respectively.

- And eventually grandchildren. (Now the circle is complete!)

John Winthrop with sons and grandsons.

JW with a well-known journalist ...

... and South Carolina governor.

John Kerry at Winthrop Roundtable.

Ambassador Barzun with JW and EGW, England, 2013.

Groton Church, Groton, England.

JW reading to Estill elementary class.

Renaissance 2013 in Charleston.

Clark

Heard

Davis

Krogh

Saint Mark's survivors (class of 1954) meet in Charleston.

OEP meeting at Ivanhoe, 2004.

Winthrop Park in Allendale, SC, 2012.

Mary Gates, Groton, England, 1983.

EGW Trip to France, 2013.

Ivanhoe, 2012.

JW at Ivanhoe, 2014.

Nathaniel T. Winthrop
with grandchildren,
circa. 1970.

John Winthrop

Date of Birth:
June 22, 1936

Education:
- Saint Mark's School (graduated "with distinction" 1954)
- Harvard College (BA 1958)
- Columbia Graduate School of Business Administration (MBA 1962)
- New York Institute of Finance (Certificate in Investment Analysis & Allied Membership)

Military Service:
- United States Navy 1958-1960 (Honorable Discharge 1964)

Employment:
- Atlantic Council of the United States (1962-1963)
- Wood, Struthers & Winthrop, Inc. (1964-1977)
- Donaldson, Lufkin & Jenrette (1977-1980)
- Chairman, deVegh Mutual Fund (1972-1980)
- Founder & President, John Winthrop & Company, Inc. (1980-Present)

Some Current Business Activities:
- Chairman, Ivanhoe Plantation, Inc., Allendale, SC (1963-Present)
- President, John Winthrop & Company, Inc. (1980-Present)

Some Past Business Activities:
- Trustee, Pioneer Funds, Boston, MA (1985-2008)
- Director, Green Bay & Western Railroad, Green Bay, WI (1970-1980)
- Trustee, Jones Heward Funds, Montreal, Canada (1970-1980)
- President and Trustee, deVegh Fund, New York, NY (1972-1980)
- Director, Donaldson, Lufkin & Jenrette, New York, NY (1977-1980)
- Director, NUI Corporation (utility company), Bedminster, NJ (1978-2002)
- Investment Company Institute, Washington, DC (1978-1981)
- Independent Trustee, Alliance Money Funds, New York, NY (1979-1996)

- ISAC Commission on Trade, Washington, DC (1984-1986)
- Board of Advisors, *Fund Directions*, New York, NY (1984-1998)
- Board of Advisors, *Board IQ*, New York, NY (2001-2008)

OTHER OUTSIDE ACTIVITIES, NOT-FOR-PROFIT:
- Trustee, Greenwich Country Day School, Greenwich, CT (1969-1974)
- Harvard Visiting Committee, Peabody, Cambridge, MA (1968-1970)
- Harvard Visiting Committee, History, Cambridge, MA (1970-1972)
- Trustee, St. Mark's School, Southborough, MA (1970-1974)
- Director, Fresh Air Fund, New York, NY (1970-1974)
- Director, The Education Policy Center, New York, NY (1977-1974)
- Director, The National Audubon Society, New York, NY (1977-1983)
- Board of Managers, Harvard Club of New York City, New York, NY (1980-1983)
- Director, Harvard Alumni Association, Elected (1984-1986)
- Director, Brookdale Foudation, New York, NY (1985-1991)
- Director, Health Sciences Foundation, Charleston, SC (1989-1991)
- Director, American Farmland Trust, Washington, DC (1992-2001)
- Director, Palmetto Project, Charleston, SC (1993-2004)
- Harvard Visiting Committee, Elected, Russian Studies, Cambridge, MA (2002-2004)
- Director, VISIONS, New York, NY (2006-Present)
- Board of Overseers, Massachusetts Historical Society, Boston, MA (2009-Present)

JOURNALISTIC EFFORTS:
- Editor, *Sierra Lookout* (1960)
- Editor, *Atlantic Community Newsletter* (1963)
- Contributed articles to *The Boston Globe, Financial Analysis Journal,* the *Wall Street Journal, Barrons, Trusts & Estates, Pension World, The New York Times* and others
- Books include "A Book of Bad Verse", "Animal Sketches", and "Letters to A Son", "Family Tree", "Scribblings", "Observations", "Picture Book", "Letters to the Editor", "Letters to Grandchildren", and "I Remember the Robins Chirping."
- And a series of books available at www.winthropfamily.org.